**MODERN
AUTO RACING
SUPERSTARS**

MODERN AUTO RACING SUPERSTARS

Ross R. Olney

Illustrated with photographs

DODD, MEAD & COMPANY
New York

PICTURE CREDITS

Goodyear Tire and Rubber Co., 55, 57, 63; Indianapolis Motor Speedway, 24, 61, 66, 99; Kensington-Koni Shocks, 83; Riverside Raceway, 107; STP, 16; Valvoline Oil Co., 11, 19, 27, 103, 105. All other photographs are by the author.

Copyright © 1978 by Ross R. Olney
All rights reserved
No part of this book may be reproduced in any form
without permission in writing from the publisher
Printed in the United States of America

1   2   3   4   5   6   7   8   9   10

Library of Congress Cataloging in Publication Data

Olney, Ross Robert, 1929-
   Modern auto racing superstars.

    Includes index.
   SUMMARY: Career biographies of Mario Andretti, James Hunt, A. J. Foyt, Niki Lauda, Bobby Allison, and Al and Bobby Unser.
   1. Automobile racing drivers—Biography—
Juvenile literature. [1. Automobile racing
drivers] I. Title.
GV1032.A1O435   796.7'2'0922 [B] [920]   78-7729
ISBN 0-396-07583-5

To **Bob, Kevin, Pat,** and **Ross** of the new **Panther Racing Team.** Good luck!

CONTENTS

INTRODUCTION 9

1 MARIO ANDRETTI 18

2 JAMES HUNT 34

3 A. J. FOYT 53

4 NIKI LAUDA 68

5 BOBBY ALLISON 81

6 AL AND BOBBY UNSER 96

INDEX 110

Mario Andretti waits before start of the 1978 Long Beach Grand Prix. He placed second and held his lead in world point standings.

INTRODUCTION

Is this right or wrong?

"Bobby Allison crawled into his Formula One racer and roared around the right-hand turn at the Indianapolis Speedway."

Or this?

"The championship Indy-type racer of Bobby Unser had an Offenhauser engine with a turbocharger."

Auto racing can seem confusing. There are so many different cars and types of racing. It is hard to tell which driver belongs to which type. Or how to tell the cars and tracks apart.

It can be easy to understand, though.

The first statement is wrong. The second one is correct. If you didn't know, you will by the end of this book. You'll read about Bobby Allison in Chapter 5. He is a *stock car* driver, not a Formula One driver. Stock cars look like ordinary passenger cars. They look like Fords, Chevrolets, and Dodges. And the Indianapolis Speedway doesn't have any right turns.

The second statement is true. Bobby Unser does drive a championship racer. His car could have a turbocharger and an Offenhauser engine. The turbocharger is a device used only on championship, Indy-type cars. It forces extra air into the engine for more power. You'll read about Bobby Unser and his Indy-type racers in this book. And about his brother, Al, too.

Racing is broken down into certain groups or types. In this book you'll find out about the following types: Formula One, championship (Indy-type), and stock cars.

There are many other types of racing cars. There are sprint cars, midget cars, Formula Two and Three cars, and even Volkswagen-powered racing cars called Formula Vee racers. There are sports cars and CanAm cars. There are

A. J. Foyt, the only four-time winner of the Indianapolis Speedway race, speeds along in his Gilmore Special, an Indy-type racer.

many, many different kinds of racing cars. Each one competes with its own kind.

The ones you will read about here are the most important ones of all. That is because the men in this book have raced their way to the top of the sport. They race only the fastest cars for the biggest prizes.

Formula One is a type of racer that races on a road course. A road course has right- and left-hand turns and faster and slower sections. Formula One races are held in any kind of weather. The cars are open-cockpit, open-wheel types like the Indy racers but they do not have turbochargers. Formula One racing is very dangerous.

Men like James Hunt, Niki Lauda, and Mario Andretti drive Formula One racers. They race on tracks like Watkins Glen in New York, Long Beach in California, Monza in Italy, and Monte Carlo in Monaco. Formula One tracks are located around the world. The names of some of the famous Formula One racing cars are McLaren, Lotus, Brabham, and Copersucar.

Formula One racers do not race at Indianapolis. Why not?

The Indianapolis speedway is not a road course, but an oval track. Indy is like Ontario Motor Speedway in California and Pocono Speedway in Pennsylvania. Indy is like many other tracks in the United States, with four "corners" and only left-hand turns. Cars like the Eagle built by Dan Gurney, the Coyote built by A. J. Foyt, and the Parnelli built by Parnelli Jones race at Indy. As fast as they are, Formula One cars would not do well at Indy. The cars that race

Niki Lauda came back from a terrible crash to win his second world championship in this Ferrari Formula One racer.

at Indy are built to race on an oval track and not on a road course.

All racing cars are very specially built. Indy cars do very well turning left, but not so well turning right. Also, they are not made to race in the rain like Formula One cars. Nobody really knows why, but that is the way it is. They always stop an Indy-type race if it starts to rain. But they allow Formula One cars to race on. The drivers just come into the pits and put special tires called "rain tires" on their racers.

Some drivers, like Mario Andretti, race both Formula One and Indy-type championship cars. But only on the right kind of tracks. Mario races Formula One racers on Formula One tracks and Indy-type championship racers on Indy-type oval tracks.

A.J. Foyt is a world-famous driver. He can drive any kind of car but he only likes to drive on oval tracks. He has won four Indy races, more than any other driver.

Foyt's Indy-type championship racers are probably the best of all. But they wouldn't do well on a road course. The Formula One-type cars would beat Foyt's cars, even with Foyt himself in the cockpit.

Why? Because Foyt's racers are built to go very fast on an oval track and Formula One cars are built to go fast on a road course.

Some American drivers like to drive stock cars. These are the cars that look like regular passenger cars. But they are really racing cars inside and out. They are rebuilt from the ground up to be as fast as possible.

Both Bobby and Al Unser are Indy drivers and also stock car drivers. Stock cars can race on almost any kind of track. But they are fastest and best on high-banked oval tracks like Daytona Speedway in Florida and Talladega Speedway in Alabama. High-banked tracks have very steep corners to help the cars speed around without spinning out or crashing. Stock cars also race on flat tracks and even on road courses like Riverside Raceway in California sometimes.

One of the best stock car drivers of all is Bobby Allison. Bobby's story is in this book. He is a champion stock car driver who also races Indy-type cars. But he does not race Formula One racers.

There are three clubs that watch over each of these three types of racing. Other groups watch over the many other types of racing. The Federation Internationale de L'Automobile is in charge of Formula One racing. The FIA is the only world-wide automobile racing club.

In the United States, the United States Auto Club watches over Indy-type championship rac-

15

One of the most famous Grand National stock cars of all is Richard Petty's red and blue No. 43.

ing. It is called USAC by racing fans. In stock car racing the main club is called NASCAR by fans. This means National Association for Stock Car Auto Racing.

Each one of these clubs has a way to pick a champion each year. Each club has a "points" system. Drivers win points in each race, depending on how well they do. The winner of each race gets the most points, of course. At the end of the racing season the points are added up and the driver with the most is the champion for that type of racing. Each year there is a USAC champion, a NASCAR champion, and a Formula One champion.

There is no overall champion, because each type of racing is so different from the other types. A driver could be the champion in two different types at the same time, but it has never happened. Once, though, a driver (Jochen Rindt) became the Formula One champion after he had been killed in a race. He had won so many points before his accident that nobody could catch up to him in the remaining races.

They do call the Formula One champion the "World Driving Champion." But that is only because Formula One tracks are scattered around the world. In this country the USAC and NASCAR champions are just as important.

Every type of racing, even the smaller events, has this points system. In this book we are most interested in the top three: Formula One, Indy-type championship racing, and stock car racing.

1
MARIO ANDRETTI

When he was a young boy, Mario Andretti dreamed of becoming a race car driver. But he lived in Italy and there was a terrible war on. His family was poor because of the war. There didn't seem much hope that he would become a world-famous racing driver.

After the war Mario moved with his family to a "relocation camp." This is a place where families go when they want to move away from the country. Mario and his twin brother, Aldo, still dreamed of being race car drivers. The family wanted to move to the United States. So did Mario and Aldo, even though they knew racing

Mario Andretti

was different here. In Italy they had road racing. In the United States, oval track racing is most popular.

But they could be race car drivers in America, they decided. Nobody paid much attention to their dreams, anyhow. It was like dreaming of being President of the United States, or a movie star.

Aldo almost succeeded as a racing champion after the family moved to the United States. He was doing fine as a driver until he had a serious accident. Then he couldn't race anymore.

Mario *did* succeed. He has become one of the most famous race car drivers in the world. Not only that, but he also is one of the most popular of all the American racing drivers.

Many times if a person becomes famous they will no longer pay attention to fans. Not Mario. He believes that the fans of auto racing are very important people. He always walks to the fence in the garage area if somebody calls his name— especially if it is a young fan calling him. Mario likes young racing fans best of all.

The road to the top was not easy for Mario Andretti. At first he raced in stock cars. These are the racers that look like regular passenger cars. But they are really race cars and very dangerous to drive.

Mario and Aldo saved their money from odd jobs and bought a racing car from the family of a racer who had been killed. This was in the 1960s and nobody would hire either boy as a driver. They began winning in their own car, then they put their winnings back into a better car. They raced around Pennsylvania where they lived. Mario still lives in Nazareth, Pennsylvania. He lives on Victory Lane, a street named in honor of his own racing career.

Mario's brother, Aldo, was injured during these early days of racing. He had to quit, but he still helps his twin brother at races.

Mario Andretti is known as an "all-out" racing driver. He drives at the ragged edge of control. He always drives as though he must win every single race.

At Indianapolis in 1969, Mario had a brand-new car. The car was owned by Andy Granatelli, who was famous as a race car builder. Many said it was the best car ever built for Indy-type racing. It had a powerful Ford engine in a body built by the Lotus company of England. The car had "four-wheel drive." Even the front wheels were turned by the engine to make the car go faster and smoother in the corners.

During practice Mario's car lost a rear wheel. He was speeding very fast at the time. The car looped out of control, smashed into a wall, and broke into many pieces. There was also a fire in the wreckage. All that was left was the cockpit section with Mario still strapped inside. He was burned and the new car was destroyed.

In only a few days the racers were going to determine their starting positions for the Indy 500. They do that by "qualification runs" to see who can go the fastest. The fastest car during these runs gets the best spot for the race. That car gets to start the race way up front. The slowest car must start the race at the back of the field on race day.

Mario had crashed his car. Oh, he had last year's older-model racer. It was called a Brawner-Hawk Special. It was a good car, everybody said. But Mario knew it wasn't as good as the one he had wrecked.

Still, it was all he had, so he made his qualification run in the older car. His burns were healing and he felt ready. With a burst of speed, he managed to go second-fastest of all thirty-three cars. Only A.J. Foyt was faster than Mario. The old car was running just fine.

In fact, Mario Andretti won the 1969 Indy 500 with the old Brawner-Hawk Special. It was a happy time in Victory Lane at the Speedway that year.

Every track has a "victory lane" where the winning car and driver are welcomed. But the one at Indy is special. Everybody who follows racing remembers when Andy Granatelli gave Mario a big kiss for winning the famous race.

Winning at Indianapolis is the dream of most American racing drivers. But nobody knew then what Mario *really* was dreaming about. Mario had won at Indy and he was a regular winner in other races. He had won stock car races, sports car races, and other types of American races. But he was thinking about something else.

"I want to win that championship so bad I can't describe it," said Mario. "I don't care if it takes 'til 1985, I'm going to win it."

The two brothers had fought their way up

Andy Granatelli gives Mario Andretti a big kiss in Victory Lane after Mario won the Indy 500 in 1969.

through the smaller, less important races. Then Mario had gone on alone to finally win many big races. He had already been the USAC Driving

Champion, so that wasn't what he was talking about. Yet that is the most important driving title in the United States. Mario had been a midget car racing champion and a sprint car racing champion, too. He was an Indy champion. What else was there to win?

Since his days as a boy in Italy, Mario had dreamed of winning the World Driving Championship. He wanted to be the champion in Formula One racers. Some say these are the most dangerous racers of all. They race on tracks around the world.

Mario didn't want to stop American-style racing, but he also wanted to be a Formula One driver.

He did it, too. Sometimes he had to travel over 200,000 miles a year to be at the races. He had to telephone his wife and three children (two boys and a girl) in Nazareth because he couldn't get home very often. But because of his skill at racing, he had become known as the "racer's racer." Even the other drivers liked him best of all.

In 1971 Mario Andretti became the first American since Dan Gurney to win a Formula One race. He won the South African Grand Prix. He also won the Questor Grand Prix that same year in California. The Questor race was a mixture of European Formula One racers and American Formula A racers. Mario was in a Ferrari Formula One racer for that race.

"To win," he said at the time, "a driver has to have inner confidence. Any driver *thinks* he can win. But deep down inside if you know the car you're driving just doesn't have it, then you're in trouble. You can't kid yourself."

Mario Andretti had become one of the three or four highest paid drivers in the world. From a displaced persons camp in Italy he had climbed to the top of the sport of motor racing. He could drive any kind of car on any kind of track in the world and win. He had proven that. Car owners tried to hire him to drive their cars. Sponsors wanted to pay him money to advertise their products.

Did Mario get a "big head?" Was he suddenly too good for the average fan?

No! Mario Andretti was still as nice as he had ever been. Ask anybody who has talked to him. They will tell you he always has time for the fans.

In Formula One racing, Mario drives the black John Player Lotus Special.

Formula One racing is different from American-style racing in another way. In America, drivers exchange information and help each other. Grand Prix (Formula One) drivers do not. Everything is a secret. If your car can go faster, you don't tell anybody why. So when Mario Andretti came along and started to help the other driver on his team, it was amazing.

But he remembered his own earlier days.

"Sure, I help, why not?" he says with a shrug.

"Lots of drivers have helped me in America when I started racing. Don Branson, in particular, helped me with dirt track racing. He taught me things that, if I'd had to learn them by myself, would have taken me six, eight months longer. I enjoy helping guys learn."

In Italy, Mario is a national hero. They remember that he was born there. But Mario loves America. He is proud that he is an American citizen. He drives for the United States. He even uses an American flag to signal his pit stops in races around the world.

In Grand Prix racing they play the national anthem of the country of the winning driver. Mario looks especially proud on the victory stand listening to "The Star-Spangled Banner" after he has won a race.

Every year Mario did better on the dangerous Formula One circuit. These world class races hurt his American racing, though. He had to travel so much, he didn't have time to practice. But more than anything else, he wanted to be the Formula One champion. So he kept trying.

He was coming closer and closer to his goal in every race. In 1976 he won the Japan Grand

Prix. The race was held during a blinding rain storm. Even the current World Champion, Niki Lauda, refused to race in that event because of the danger.

Mario switched from one racing team to another, trying to do better. He raced for the Lotus company in England, for Ferrari in Italy, and for Parnelli Jones' American racing team. Then he switched back to Lotus again.

Very few drivers in the world are ranked by the FIA to race in Formula One. It sometimes takes years before a driver has worked his way up to Formula One. Usually only about twenty-five drivers are good enough for this type of racing. Very few of *them* make much money racing. But Mario Andretti has become rich as a racing driver.

He won the Long Beach Grand Prix in 1977, a race through the city streets. He passed Jody Scheckter on the next-to-last lap. Then he flew directly to Spain and won the next Grand Prix Formula One race in Madrid. Not many drivers have won two in a row in this type of racing.

Suddenly Mario was in second place in the points standings for 1977. He had a chance at

Victory Lane at the Long Beach Grand Prix in 1977. Mario Andretti called it one of his highest moments in racing.

his dream; he could win the World Driving Championship.

So he drove at the peak of his skill. He *never* gave up. His race at Dijon, France, was an example. At the start Mario dropped back to third place. But then he drove as fast as he could. He passed the second-place car and then began to try to pass the leader, John Watson. But Watson held him off for lap after lap. Mario continued to try to pass. On every curve of every lap he would pull up directly behind the racer of Watson. But wherever he went, Watson was there first.

Watson's car was faster on the straightaways of the track. So the leader would pull ahead there. Then, in the turns, Mario would close up behind him. The race was nearing an end. Mario needed the victory to hold second place in the points standings. He tried again and again to pass Watson.

Finally, on the final turn of the last lap, he threw caution to the wind. With Watson's car struggling and almost out of gas, Mario sped forward. He barely skimmed around the leader and pulled into the lead himself just as the checkered flag was falling.

Mario (car No. 9) leads the field in the 1977 California 500 for Indy-type racers. Next to him (No. 21) is Al Unser.

Mario Andretti had won his fifth Grand Prix. Few other American drivers had ever done so well. Only one other American driver, Phil Hill, had ever won the Formula One championship. That had been nearly twenty years before.

Mario did not win the championship in 1977. He won the Italian Grand Prix later that year. But then he began to have car problems that kept him from winning the remaining races. He finally finished high enough to be in third place in the points standings. It was a good position, but not good enough for Mario. Everybody believes that sooner or later he will be the World Driving Champion.

Most American fans hope so.

It would be good for America once again to have an American as the World Champion in auto racing. Mario Andretti has won in every other type of racing he has tried. He was thirty-seven years old in 1977, a veteran driver with great experience behind the wheel. He is good at what he does, one of the best in the world.

If anybody can win the championship for the United States, Mario Andretti can.

2
JAMES HUNT

The sky was very dark over the speedway at the base of Mount Fuji in Japan. The snowy top of the tall mountain was hidden in mist. It had been raining and more rain was sure to come. The fog was heavy on the track. Auto racing is always dangerous, but it is most dangerous in the rain.

Only Grand Prix cars race in the rain. Other types of racers come into the pits and wait for the track to dry. But Formula One Grand Prix cars just change tires and keep racing.

So every fan knew that this race would go on even in bad weather. But it would be dangerous for the drivers.

James Hunt

For two of them this was to be the most important race of their lives. Last year's World Driving Champion, Niki Lauda, could be the champion again. All he had to do was finish this race in the top ten. Even if he didn't win, he would earn enough points to keep the championship. Lauda was an Austrian driver, driving a blood-red Italian Ferrari racing car.

Only one other racer could possibly take the championship from Lauda. He was a good-looking young driver. Many said he looked just like a racing driver should look. He had long blond hair and a broad grin. He loved driving racing cars. He was a winner in many other sports, a natural athlete, but racing was his favorite sport.

He seemed to have no fear. He laughed at danger like driving fast cars on a wet track. He would win the championship if he could place third or better, no matter what Lauda did.

His name was James Hunt. He was an Englishman.

That 1976 Japan Grand Prix at Fujiyama was won by the American driver, Mario Andretti. Andretti had no fear either. He drove very fast through the cold, blinding rain to win. Many drivers lost control on the wet track and spun out. Others crashed. But not Andretti.

And not James Hunt. He didn't win but he didn't crash, either.

Former champion Niki Lauda had been badly hurt in a race only a few weeks before. He drove into the pits and out of the race in Japan after only a few laps. It was a very important race to him, but he dropped out.

"It is too dangerous," he said. With that, he gave up the World Championship.

James Hunt, a devil-may-care driver, raced on in the gloom in his fast McLaren Special. He tried to catch Mario Andretti, but he could not. Still, by the end of the race, he was in third place. That earned him just enough points. James Hunt was the new World Driving Champion, the best Formula One driver in the world.

Many said he was an ideal champion that year of 1976. For the entire year he flew about the world, racing, making speeches, telling people about auto racing. He was an expert trumpet player. He was a champion tennis player and a fine squash player. He dressed in expensive clothes. He looked like a winner.

As Hunt lowers himself into his McLaren, team manager Teddy Mayer makes last-minute notes.

Hunt loved being the champion. He was always smiling and happy, for he had won the title he set out to win.

It seemed easy for James Hunt, but it was not always so easy. For many years he had tried to win in auto racing but he failed. Only a year or so before, he had been almost unknown. Nearly thirty years old, his life appeared to be a failure.

Perhaps James Hunt should have done what he first planned to do. He decided to become a doctor after high school. The son of a wealthy stockbroker, he attended one of the better-known public schools in England. At Wellington College in Shropshire he was on the team in almost every sport. But still he did not want to go into sports as a full-time job. He wanted to go on to medical school. James Hunt would probably have made a fine doctor.

One day he visited the Silverstone Race Track in England. He watched the speeding cars race around the track. Deep inside he was very excited.

"I can do that," the young man thought to himself.

So James asked his father to give him his college money to buy a racing car. "No!" said Hunt's father. Racing, the father knew, was a dangerous sport. He still wanted his son to be a doctor.

But James Hunt had made up his mind. Instead of going to school, the eighteen-year-old Hunt started working at odd jobs around the race track. With his snapping blue eyes and ready smile he could talk others into giving him jobs. He saved his money. Nobody paid much attention to the blond young man with the wide smile who said he was going to be a racer. But that didn't stop James Hunt.

Soon he had enough money to buy a used racing car. The trouble was, the car was quickly turned down by officials at the track. The tires were smooth. Hunt tried to tell them that the tires were his special "secret weapon" but they didn't believe him. They just believed that he didn't have enough money to buy good tires. And they were right. They would not allow him to race the old car.

Hunt was sad, but he didn't give up. By working even harder he saved enough money to buy a Formula Ford racing car. This is not the fastest class of racer, but at least Hunt could finally enter some races.

Racing was a tough business, he quickly learned.

"I always seemed to be involved in other people's accidents," he said. By the time he had worked his way up into Formula Three racing, a faster type, he had been nicknamed "Hunt the Shunt."

A *shunt* in racing is a crash. James Hunt crashed many times. Soon nobody would allow him to drive in any races. Racing fans forgot about James Hunt, the one who always crashed.

But an English nobleman, Lord Alexander Hesketh, did not forget the young, wild driver. He had been watching James Hunt and he liked what he saw. Hunt had courage. Hesketh had always wanted to be a part of auto racing as a car owner. But he was new, with a new car. He couldn't get any of the famous drivers to drive for him.

"Nobody wanted to drive for me and nobody wanted James Hunt to drive for him. We were obviously meant for each other," said Lord Hesketh. He hired James Hunt to drive his new Formula Two car. Formula Two is next to Formula One, the fastest cars in world class racing.

Hunt continued to crash. But Hesketh was rich. He had enough money to repair the car, and they kept trying and trying. It seemed to be no use. They couldn't win a race.

Meanwhile, James Hunt was learning to be a racing driver. Finally, Lord Hesketh made an unusual decision.

"We had failed at everything else. There was nowhere to hide. We decided we might as well move *upwards.*"

Upward they moved, into Formula One racing. Formula One is fast, exciting, very dangerous auto racing. Many famous drivers have died during Formula One races. This type of racing costs a lot of money, too. Hesketh started out by renting a Surtees Formula One racing car. He entered James Hunt in the 1973 "Race of Champions" at Brands Hatch Circuit in Kent, England.

Suddenly all of Hunt's experience seemed to pay off. He felt *good* in the new Formula One car. He came in third in the race. It was a fine finish for a young driver. He hadn't crashed and he had almost *won.* James Hunt was on his way in big-time motor racing.

By 1974 the Hesketh Racing Team had their own racing car and James Hunt won some major

James Hunt pulls on his fire-resistant suit before a Formula One race.

races. In 1975, Hunt won the Dutch Grand Prix, his first Formula One race that earned points toward the championship. He finished fourth in championship points that year. Never again would the fans forget James Hunt (though many still called him "Shunt," for he still crashed at times).

Along the way, Hunt's temper would sometimes show. During the Long Beach Grand Prix in 1976, he bumped against the racer of Frenchman Patrick Depailler. Depailler's car went on in the race. Hunt's car spun around and crashed. Hunt was not hurt. He jumped out of his car full of anger.

Walking boldly down the middle of the race track, with speeding cars all around, he waited for Patrick Depailler. As the Frenchman's car sped past, Hunt raised his fist and shook it. He paid no attention to the other cars inches away from him. Later the two drivers met in the pressroom and shouted bitterly at each other. Each blamed the other for the crash. This sometimes happens in auto racing.

In another auto race, Hunt was fined by the FIA for doing the same thing. Nobody is allowed to walk on a race track, not even a driver. It is much too dangerous.

James Hunt wanted to win the World Driving Championship more than anything else. But he was having trouble on the track and in his personal life as well. His wife didn't care for the danger of motor racing. She left him. Lord Hesketh decided that racing was costing too much money. He dropped out. Hunt was out of a job. He had no car to race.

Just when things looked worst for James Hunt, McLaren driver Emerson Fittipaldi decided he wanted to drive a car from Brazil. Fittipaldi was from Brazil so he wanted a Brazilian car to win.

The McLaren racer from England needed a new driver. The McLaren team had one of the best cars in racing and one of the best crews of mechanics. With James Hunt holding his breath and waiting, McLaren team manager Teddy Mayer looked over the out-of-work drivers. He chose Hunt. Hunt knew he would have to try very hard to keep the job.

In his very first race of 1976, Hunt put the McLaren racer "on the pole," the fastest car of all during qualifications. He didn't win that first race, but he drove very well.

He was second behind World Champion Niki Lauda in the South African Grand Prix. Then he won two nonchampionship (no points awarded) races in England. Finally he won his first Grand Prix for McLaren in Spain. The McLaren team was jumping around in happiness. But the James Hunt bad luck was about to strike again.

While he was getting his trophy from the King of Spain, race inspectors were examining his racer. They didn't like what they found. Formula One racers are built to very tight rules. They said Hunt's car was a half-inch too wide. It was against the rules. Hunt found himself to be the only Grand Prix winner ever to have his victory taken away from him.

There were meetings and more meetings as unhappy James Hunt waited. Newspaper reporters buzzed around, expecting the final word from the top officials. It came. Niki Lauda, who had placed second in the race, was awarded the victory.

By the time the McLaren team arrived in France for the next race, James Hunt had only *eight points.* Nobody gave Hunt much chance to win the championship that year, he was so far behind.

But James didn't give up. He knew the way to win the championship was to win races. He still thought he could be the champ. He won the French Grand Prix. Then, one day later, a Paris court gave him back his victory in the Spanish Grand Prix. The judge said Hunt's McLaren racer was legal after all. The very next week, Hunt won the British Grand Prix. He was really *racing!*

Feeling much better about everything, the McLaren team of driver and mechanics hurried to Germany. The German Grand Prix was the next race. Hunt led every single lap of the race and won easily. Nobody was happy, though—especially James Hunt. For during the race a terrible accident happened.

Niki Lauda, the leader in points standings, had crashed and burned. His car had been struck by another, then other cars had hit him. Nobody could stop in time. Lauda was very badly hurt and not expected to live. Everybody was sad, for Niki Lauda was a popular driver.

What did James Hunt do? He and Niki were pals even if they did race each other. Worried and sad, Hunt rushed to the hospital to be with his friend. Lauda fought for his life as James Hunt waited.

Finally the doctors said that Lauda would live. So James Hunt went to Holland to race in the Dutch Grand Prix. Even if they are sad about an accident, racing men go ahead and race. It is their job. It is their life. On his twenty-ninth birthday, James Hunt won the Dutch Grand Prix in his speeding McLaren.

By then he had won 56 points. Lauda had 61, but everybody thought he was out of racing forever. Hunt had an excellent chance to win the driving championship. Only four weeks before it had seemed impossible.

Then bad luck hit Hunt again. On his way to the United States and Canada for the next two races, he was told that he had lost another race in the courts. The British Grand Prix had been taken away from him. They said he had not re-entered the race correctly after a crash. People in England didn't like it, but that is the way it was. The judges gave the victory to hospitalized

James Hunt's 1977 McLaren was one of the fastest cars on the Formula One circuit.

Niki Lauda, who had placed second in the race. That gave Niki more points. And it took away points from James Hunt.

Still, Hunt did not give up. He had had some bad luck, yes. But he decided to try as hard as he could to win more races. He could make up the points if he could win enough times.

He won both the United States Grand Prix at Watkins Glen and the Canadian Grand Prix. He was living a very dangerous life, but the points score drew closer again. It was Hunt 65, Lauda 68. How could Lauda have 68 points? The amazing Niki had come back from his terrible accident. He was racing again in spite of his injuries.

There was one race left to run that year of 1976. It was to be the Japan Grand Prix on the slopes of Mount Fuji. That race has become a part of the folklore of auto racing.

There were floods and fog and rain in Japan. It was one of the most dangerous races ever run. Many drivers simply dropped out, unable to see the track.

With only five laps to go in the race, James Hunt seemed to have the championship in his hands. Mario Andretti was leading, but Hunt was in third place. That was all he needed to win the overall championship. Lauda had already dropped out. Hunt was racing along in the rain with a great spray of water from his wheels. But then the track began to dry out and Hunt's tires were wrong. They were built for running on a wet track, not a dry one. They began to fail.

Finally he had to rush into the pits for a change. Once again it seemed that Niki Lauda was to win the championship, for Hunt *had* to place third to go ahead.

Even then the battling James Hunt did not give up.

He roared back onto the track with new tires. He drove as fast as he could. He paid no attention at all to the danger. He passed some other racers to move into fifth place. He battled his way around Swiss driver Clay Regazzoni to take fourth place. He finally moved around Alan Jones into third place. The race was almost over.

Hunt didn't even know he was in third place, so he drove on as fast as ever. At the end of the race he didn't believe he was in third place. He didn't believe it when his pit men told him. But then finally, with people clapping him on the back and calling him "Champ," the famous grin crossed his face.

He knew that he was the 1976 World Driving Champion. It had taken years to work up to Formula One. Then it had taken ten months of

James Hunt racing in the 1978 Long Beach Grand Prix

hard, dangerous driving and more than 3,000 miles on the race track. He had won the championship from Niki Lauda by *one single point,* the closest in the history of racing.

But he was the champion, no doubt about that.

The world of auto racing was pleased for James Hunt. The fans knew that Hunt had won his championship because he just wouldn't give up, no matter what happened.

3
A.J. FOYT

Racing fans gave Anthony Joseph Foyt many nicknames. Most called him "A.J." But he is also called "Super Tex" and "Tough Tony."

They gave him these fancy nicknames because he is probably the best driver in the history of auto racing.

At least in American-style racing. That is what Texan A.J. Foyt does best. He has won races in Europe, but only for the fun of it. Foyt races at Indianapolis and at all the other American tracks. He has won every major race at least once and every championship in every type of

American racer he has tried.

Yes, Foyt started racing early in life. When he was only six years old his father built him a small racer.

"It was the most beautiful thing I ever saw," Foyt remembers. It wasn't long before young A.J. was racing at the local track. When he was only eleven years old, he raced against adults. Sometimes he beat them, too.

A.J. came up the hard way. He had to race for little money on poor tracks. There were other young drivers trying to work their way up, too. Some didn't make it, but Foyt reached the top.

He visited the Indianapolis Speedway five times before he raced there. He sat in the grandstands and watched the other drivers. Foyt knew it was a good way to learn.

Finally, in 1958, he raced for the first time at Indy. But it was an unhappy race for everybody. Foyt finished in 16th place. He spun out on lap 148 of the 200-lap race. Nobody remembers Foyt that year because of what happened at the start of the race.

There was a terrible accident on the first lap in the third turn. Fifteen racers were involved. Sev-

A. J. Foyt

eral were completely wrecked and driver Pat O'Connor was killed.

In fact, thirteen of the racing drivers in A.J. Foyt's first Indy race have died in racing cars. Auto racing is a very dangerous sport.

A.J. Foyt became famous for many reasons. He won the Daytona 500-mile race for stock cars. That is the main race for this type of racer. He won European sports car races. He has won so many dirt track races for midget racers and sprint car racers that keeping score is hard. He has been the USAC National Driving Champion six times, far more than any other driver.

But he is most famous for winning at the Indianapolis Speedway. Many drivers race at Indy and never win. They race again and again, but victory never comes. They keep racing there because Indianapolis is considered to be the best race of all to win. If a driver wins at the famous Speedway, he is set for life. He will earn money from then on for advertising products. He will never have to fight to get a good race car to drive. His name will be important in racing.

So drivers keep trying and trying to win the Indy race, but most fail.

Foyt and 1925 winner, Peter DePaolo, the oldest living former winner of the Indy 500.

A.J. Foyt did not fail. He succeeded beyond the dreams of any driver.

After skidding out of the 1958 Indy race, Foyt raced on other tracks. But it was the Indy race he most wanted to win. He came back the following year and placed 10th in the big 500-mile race. In 1960 he dropped to a 25th-place finish because of car problems.

A.J. Foyt was not doing well at the race every

driver most wants to win. Not until 1961. In that race the tables were turned.

It had been a race-long battle with another young driver, "Fast Eddie" Sachs. First Foyt would lead, then Sachs would lead. Both drivers were very popular with the fans, so the shouting and cheering was long and loud.

With final pit stops for fuel already made, the race seemed to be going all the way to the finish. Then Foyt got some bad news from his pit. His last pit stop had not been right. The fuel had not been pumped properly and he was going to run dry.

"COME IN" ordered the pit sign as Foyt flashed by on the straightaway. His heart sank. He had been sure he was going to beat Sachs.

By the time he added gas and came back on the track, Sachs was several seconds ahead. But A.J. didn't give up. He drove faster and faster, forcing Fast Eddie to new speeds.

Suddenly the luck that had been Fast Eddie's switched to A.J., for Eddie was motioning to a tire as he passed his own pit. The high speeds had worn out a tire on Sachs' racer. Fast Eddie hurried into his pit for a new tire as Foyt thundered by on the track. At the end of the race, A.J. Foyt was 8 seconds ahead of Eddie Sachs. A.J. had won his first Indianapolis Speedway race. It was not to be his last.

Some people say that Foyt has a quick temper. They say he is sometimes difficult to get along with. But Foyt is a man who cannot bear to lose a race. When he has won he is easygoing and happy. He will talk to reporters and sign autographs.

When he loses a race he just wants to be alone. He cannot seem to wait for the next race so he can win again. The more famous Foyt became, the more people followed him around. At the race track it became very difficult even to see Foyt because of the crowds of people.

Off the track he is just like everybody else and nicer than most. Once he was driving to a race and he stopped to help an elderly woman. Her car had a flat tire and she didn't know what to do. Foyt fixed her tire and then drove on. She never knew that her tire had been repaired by the most famous driver in racing history.

The year 1964 was not a happy year at Indy. Some of the drivers were in new rear-engined racers. But Foyt didn't like the new cars. He decided to drive his old faithful roadster with the engine in the front. He liked the older car, and trusted it.

In the second lap of the race, driver Dave MacDonald skidded into the fourth turn wall. His burning car bounced back in the middle of the track. By then it seemed like everything was burning. Coming full speed directly behind was Fast Eddie Sachs, also in one of the new-type cars.

Eddie smashed into MacDonald's racer and both cars exploded. Both drivers were killed.

After the wreckage was cleared, Foyt drove to his second victory at the Indianapolis Speedway.

"It hurts when you lose friends," Foyt said afterward. "We have feelings like everybody else. You want to park your car and chuck your helmet in the cockpit and walk away. But this is our business. Death and injury are part of the sport. We all live with it."

A.J. Foyt was nearing a record that only three other drivers in history had managed. But the way was not easy. In January, 1965, he had a serious accident at Riverside International

Foyt's racer is on the pole for the start of the 1965 Indy 500. Directly behind Foyt is Mario Andretti and beside him is eventual winner, Jim Clark.

Raceway in California. His stock car bounced high into the air. It landed upside down and pinned A.J. inside the wreckage.

When rescue workers cut him free, he had a crushed foot and a broken bone in his back. Yet only three months later he entered another stock car race. He was limping and in pain, but he drove as well as ever. He finally won that race.

In the 1967 Indy 500 there was another strange new machine. It was the turbine-powered racer of former winner Parnelli Jones. The car didn't roar, it *hissed.* It was more like a jet plane than a racing car. Everybody thought it would win.

Everybody but Foyt. He thought it would break down before the 500-mile race was over. So he decided to race for second place and be there to win when the turbine broke down. It was risky strategy, but it worked.

On lap 197 the turbine failed and Foyt swept ahead. On the last lap of that race Foyt had to steer through a five-car smashup on the mainstraightaway. But he did it to win the Indy race for the *third* time. Only three other drivers had ever done that.

No man had ever won the Indy race four times. A.J. Foyt was sure he could. So he tried for ten years through crashes, mechanical problems, and other hardships. Foyt was trying to build a new racer. He had designed and built the new car himself, and named it "Coyote."

Foyt poses with his famous Coyote racing car, an Indy-type racer with a turbocharger.

It takes time for a new racer to be perfected. Foyt came close to winning some 500-mile races, but his luck didn't hold out. He was winning other races, though. When A.J. Foyt enters a race he is always considered a favorite to win. He can drive any type of racer on any type of track.

He just couldn't seem to win again at Indy. But

the record of the ten years improved. In 1971 and again in 1975 he placed third. Then in 1976 he placed second. He was getting very close to seeing his dream come true.

Many years ago, in 1936, a driver by the name of Lou Meyer won the Indy race for the third time. He raced for a few more years but he never won there again. In 1940 Wilbur Shaw won for the third time. He never won again. In 1948 Mauri Rose won the Indy 500 for the third time. He never won again either.

A.J. Foyt had won the Indy race for the third time in 1967. People asked him when he was going to retire from racing. He was racing new, young drivers. He was racing the sons of some of the fathers he had raced in the beginning.

"As long as my eyes hold out I'm going to keep right on racing. That's the key to being a good race driver," he would say. But most people thought it was because he wanted to win the Indy 500 one more time. He wanted to be the only man in history ever to win the famous race four times.

Then came 1977. It was a fine race before the largest crowd in sports history. More than

350,000 people jammed the old Speedway and millions more watched on TV. The most famous drivers in racing were there, including A.J. Foyt. And including the first woman driver ever to race at Indy, Janet Guthrie.

It was a happy, excited crowd and it was a fine race. Before it was halfway over the race had settled down to a battle between A.J. Foyt, Gordon Johncock, and Al Unser. Driver after driver pulled sadly into the pits with mechanical problems. Others crashed into the walls.

The lady driver, Janet Guthrie, sat out most of the race in the pits with car problems.

Finally it was Foyt against Johncock and the lead switched back and forth. But as the race neared an end, the strain on Johncock's engine was too much. It exploded and the driver parked his car at the end of the main straightaway.

Moments later A.J. Foyt took the checkered flag. He had won his *fourth* Indy race. He was the only driver ever to do so. He was very happy as he guided his racer into Victory Lane.

"We did it . . . we did it . . . " he said over and over again. The owner of the Speedway was weeping with happiness. Foyt had always been

Victory Lane at Indy for the *fourth* time. Foyt waves to the fans as the checkered-shirt pit crew clusters around. Smiling broadly, directly to Foyt's right, is his father, Tony, Sr.

like a son to Tony Hulman, the owner.

Then the radio and television announcers pressed forward. They pushed their microphones at A.J.

"Is this it, A.J.?" they shouted over the din. "Are you going to retire?"

Foyt looked around. He was happier than he had ever been. He loved where he was. He loved the crowd and the noise and the speed. He loved victory more than anything else.

"I think I'll try for number *five,*" he said with a grin.

4
NIKI LAUDA

It was a terrible racing accident. It happened in 1976 at Nürburgring, a famous Formula One race track in Germany. The driver in the wreck was an Austrian by the name of Andreas Nikilaus Lauda.

He was better known in racing as "Niki" Lauda. In fact, he was one of the best-known drivers in the world. He was the 1975 World Driving Champion. In the dangerous Formula One racers he had earned more points than any other driver that year.

Most fans expected him to be the 1976 champion until that race at Nürburgring. After that,

Niki Lauda

nobody expected him to ever be the champion again. But he fooled them.

Lauda is a small man. He is slight of build and quick moving. He speaks rapidly in the several languages he knows. Many fans say he has a mind like a computer. He becomes almost a part of his machine in a race.

At Nürburgring Lauda was racing up a short straightaway and into a shallow left-hand turn. His car seemed to be running well and he felt good. Coming quickly behind him was an American, Brett Lunger. Lunger saw Lauda's car fly off the track for no apparent reason. Something had broken and Lauda could no longer steer the speeding racer.

Lauda's Ferrari bounced and ripped through two fences. Then it skidded up a steep bank by the side of the track. That bounced it back onto the track. Burning, it came to a stop in front of the other racers.

Instantly Lunger's car slammed into Lauda's car. That spread the fire to Lunger. Driver Harold Ertl then hit Lauda. The track was full of burning wreckage. Lunger jumped from his car and tried to help Lauda escape.

In the cockpit, Lauda is said to become almost a part of the racer. He doesn't seem to recognize the "outside world."

Meanwhile, driver Art Merzario stopped his racer and ran into the flames to help. But the fire flared up and the two drivers were forced away. Then fire fighters moved in to try to smother the flames with foam. The two drivers came back in. They could see that Lauda was conscious. He was trying to unhook his seat belts.

In spite of the fire, Lunger leaped on top of the Ferrari and pulled up on Lauda's shoulders. Merzario unhooked the belts and the men tumbled to the flaming track. Drivers of racing cars are brave in the races. They are also very brave in emergencies. They always try to help each other in a crash.

The three drivers ran away from the flames. Lunger wasn't hurt. Niki Lauda was very badly hurt. His helmet had ripped away in the crash and he had broken bones in his face. His face was also seriously burned. But worst of all, he had breathed in poison fumes and fire during the crash. His lungs were very badly hurt.

Three days later, Niki Lauda was given last rites by a priest from his church. Everyone thought he was dying. Nobody believed they would ever see him alive again.

But fans did see him again. Doctors couldn't believe what was happening. Lauda refused to give up. He was in terrible pain but he wouldn't stay in bed. He was back in a racing car in only six weeks.

He couldn't wear his regular size helmet because of the bandages on his head. So he wore a larger helmet. The bandages were to protect skin grafts. The trouble was, he was losing his championship to British driver James Hunt. If he

Lauda's Ferrari is perhaps the finest Formula One racer in the world.

didn't start racing again, he would lose it for sure. While he had been in the hospital, Hunt had been winning.

At Nürburgring Lauda had been 30 points ahead. By the time he came to his next race in Italy, he was leading by only 2 points.

Everybody was surprised and happy to see Niki. Lauda is one of the most popular drivers in Formula One racing. The other drivers all like and respect him, for he is the best. They did not like to see the scars from his crash. But they were more than pleased that he did not die.

Lauda was his old self. He had known that he would be back. He had known that the doctors were wrong. He knew the priest had come too soon.

"My philosophy and way of thinking about motor racing have not changed a bit since the accident," he said. He planned to fight for his championship just like always.

If everybody thought he was brave, they would learn that he was brave in more ways than one. He came back to race even though he was in great pain. But three races later he did something that took almost as much courage.

The next two races were even. Lauda was driving as well as he always did. In his clipped German accent, he said, "I will again be the former Lauda, the usual Lauda, willing to run because he knows he can win . . . as he is the fastest."

The last race of 1976 was in Japan. The score before the race was Lauda 68 points, James Hunt 65. It seemed that Lauda would again be the champion in spite of his accident only a few

Niki Lauda leads Ronnie Peterson, who is driving the strange-looking, six-wheeled Elf Tyrrel racer.

weeks before. All he had to do was finish in the top ten.

American Mario Andretti won that Japan Grand Prix. James Hunt placed third and became the new World Driving Champion. For Niki Lauda had simply pulled out of the race. It was raining and foggy and nobody could see very well. His own eyes, still healing from the burns to his face, were failing him.

"There is more than just the championship," he said softly after pulling his Ferrari into the pits. He had only raced two laps when he made his choice to quit. "There is life," he explained. "I am a normal human being, not crazy. There is nothing wrong with the car. I'm just not going to drive like an idiot when I don't see a thing. I don't care what people say about my decisions."

It took courage to pull out of the race. But Niki had done so with the whole racing world watching.

Surely, many fans thought, his career is at an end. Surely he will lose his job with Ferrari.

In London, England, Lauda was given an award for bravery by the Victoria Sporting Club.

As quiet and modest as always, he spoke to the club members. "I'm no hero. There are two elements that make up valor. One is skill. The other is dashing personal courage. Of course dashing personal courage is more spectacular. In my career, skill and practice have always outweighed personal courage by far.

"Practice makes perfect," he concluded.

Niki Lauda did not think he was finished with racing. His boss, Commendatore Enzo Ferrari, did not think so either. The Commendatore stood behind Niki. He defended Lauda's right to pull out of a dangerous race if he didn't feel he could drive in it.

The Ferrari is one of the best Formula One racers in the world. Most drivers would like to drive a Ferrari. Niki Lauda was offered the driving job again in 1977.

He was still not like the other drivers. Most Formula One drivers are strong, outgoing, romantic men and women. They are the center of attention wherever they go. They attract crowds. They enjoy the fact that they are well-known and popular. They make fine speeches and tell good jokes. They speak several languages and are usually very intelligent people.

Lauda is very intelligent too. But he is quiet and dedicated to racing. He would rather be with his car than with people. He would rather fly his airplane alone than attend a party, even if he is the guest of honor. They call him a "mechanical man" and in some ways the name fits him.

Formula One drivers begin their careers in

Waiting by his car, Lauda is quiet and tries to avoid fans and photographers.

different ways. Today, a driver must bring a sponsor with him to a racing team. He must offer the car owner enough money to make the deal worthwhile. Then if the driver wins, other sponsors will come. He doesn't have to worry about that part of the business anymore.

A brand-new driver has a problem. No sponsor wants to give him any money. He has not proven he can win. So he must sponsor himself. He must "buy" a ride with his own money.

That should have been easy for Niki Lauda. His father was a wealthy paper mill owner in Austria. But Niki's father didn't want Niki to be a race driver. He said, "No."

Niki came up with a new plan. Nobody had thought of it before. He went to a bank and borrowed enough money to attract a car owner. But when you borrow money, you must offer some "security" to the bank. Niki offered them his life insurance policy. So he was the only driver ever to mortgage his own life to get into racing.

At first it was very difficult for Niki. He didn't have good race cars and he didn't win many races. But when he joined Ferrari he began to win.

So Lauda remained with Ferrari after he pulled out of the 1976 Japan Grand Prix. In 1977 he began to win races again. Throughout the year he was high in the points standings. As the 1977 season drew to a close several drivers were battling for the new championship.

Mario Andretti was high in the standings. So was South African driver Jody Scheckter, a young driver of great promise. Other drivers had collected many points during the season.

But one driver had won the championship with several races yet to go. He had earned enough championship points during the season so that no other driver could catch him. This was a driver who many fans thought would never race again.

Strapped in the cockpit of his blood-red Ferrari, with shiny burn scars across his face, he was better than ever. He was the 1977 World Driving Champion, as he had been the 1975 champion.

He was twenty-eight-year-old Niki Lauda, a driver who had come roaring back after an accident that almost took his life.

5
BOBBY ALLISON

Close finishes are standard in NASCAR stock car racing. The Yankee 400 at Michigan International Speedway was a good example. The year was 1971.

In the Coca-Cola Mercury stock car was one of racing's best drivers, Bobby Allison. In the Petty Plymouth was the "king" of stock cars, Richard Petty. The two drivers switched the lead back and forth time after time. By lap 174 of the 197-lap race, the battle had become a side-by-side duel that had the fans standing and cheering.

First it would be Allison, then Petty. Then the

next time around it would be Allison in the lead again. The two drivers were trying as hard as they could to beat each other.

Stock cars are very popular among the fans. The cars look like real passenger cars. They seem to be the same cars as those out in the parking lot. But they are not. They are racing cars just like any other racer. They are built from the ground up to be racers.

Still, they look like regular cars, so that makes the races very exciting. A Ford owner wants a Ford car to win, even if he knows it is a racing car. A Plymouth owner is happy when a Plymouth look-alike wins.

The two drivers, Allison and Petty, continued their great race at Michigan Speedway. Fender to fender, they roared along. One would gain a few feet, then the other. They were equal in power and skill.

On lap 193 Richard Petty pulled slightly ahead. But on lap 195 Bobby Allison drove down low on the track and raced past Petty. Petty dropped in close behind.

On lap 197, the last lap, Petty tried to move around Allison. He pressed down hard on his

Bobby Allison

gas pedal and pulled almost up beside the Coca-Cola Special. But Allison stepped on his own gas and held the lead.

"I figured Richard would try to come under me off number four turn," Allison explained later. "Once I got into that fourth turn, I knew I had him."

The two roaring cars raced under the checkered flag. Allison was one car-length ahead. His winnings were more than $15,000 for that race alone.

Racing like that is what earned Bobby Allison one of the sport's highest honors. In 1972 he was selected auto racing's "Driver of the Year." To win the award, he had to beat out drivers like George Follmer, Bobby Unser, and Mark Donohue. He also had to beat A.J. Foyt, Joe Leonard, and the same Richard Petty. The award, called the "Golden Eagles" prize, is given by a group of automotive sportswriters. Another group, the American Auto Racing Writers and Broadcasters Association, also gave Bobby an award. He was voted to their "All America" team of the best drivers in the country.

Bobby Allison drives other cars, too. He is best

known in stock car racing, but he is also well known as an Indy-car driver. Most stock car drivers do not do well in Indy cars, but Allison does. He is a natural racing driver, able to drive most any race car.

In stock car racing, Bobby Allison is a superstar. Close finishes like the race at Michigan Speedway happen very often in stock cars. And very often it seems that Bobby Allison is involved. Sometimes he wins, sometimes he loses. No matter which, he tries harder than most other drivers.

In a hard-fought stock car race at Riverside International Raceway in California, Bobby was leading. He was fighting for the lead with his own brother, Donnie. At the end of the race, Donnie had beaten Bobby by less than one car-length. To make the race even more exciting, driver Buddy Baker was only three feet behind Bobby as the race ended.

At another stock car race in Michigan, David Pearson beat Bobby Allison by less than one car-length. This was after a 400-mile battle.

At Trenton, New Jersey, Bobby Allison beat Bobby Isaac by 1.4 seconds at the end of a

Allison thunders his Matador stock car down the straightaway at Riverside past another car.

300-mile race. He beat David Pearson by a couple of lengths at Darlington, South Carolina, after a wild race of 500 miles.

Stock car racing is fast, exciting, and usually very close. Most stock cars end the race with scrapes and dings on the body. During the race the cars touch each other very often. This is dangerous at high speed, but it happens all the time.

One crew chief on a NASCAR stock car said what most fans believe. "I feel we have the best driver in Bobby Allison. He can race all day long and race as fast on the last lap as he did on the first. Bobby doesn't ever let down, from the green to the checkered flag."

Bobby Allison began NASCAR racing in 1961. He had always wanted to be a race car driver. At first it was hard because he didn't have the best cars and he was new. But he began to gain experience as a racer in stock cars.

He became very, very good in the "Sportsman" division of stock car racing. These are older stock cars but still very fast. Then Bobby began to win some races in the "Grand National" division of stock car racing. These are the newest, fastest cars.

Stock car drivers make good money if they finish well at all. But certain ones make more than the others. In 1974 Bobby Allison became a millionaire driver in NASCAR. Richard Petty was the only other millionaire driver at that time. Allison has won more than 400 races in his career, including more than 50 on the rich NASCAR circuit of tracks.

The Allison name is well known in stock car racing for another reason. Among Bobby's three brothers is Donnie Allison. Donnie may not yet be a superstar like his brother, but he is an excellent driver who wins many races.

Bobby Allison also has five sisters who cheer him on during his races. So there are plenty of Allisons around when most stock car races are held. The announcer at the track sometimes mixes them up, there are so many.

Once when Bobby was driving for race car owner Roger Penske, he had trouble with his engine. It was serious trouble and he pulled into the pits at Riverside. The CAM 2 Matador Special was popping, banging, and smoking. Mechanics looked under the hood, then shook their heads.

It was no use. They couldn't fix the engine in time. It looked like they were out for the day.

But Bobby Allison wouldn't quit. Getting some help, he pushed the car behind the pit wall. Then he asked Roger Penske to *change* the engine. He was in the middle of a fast race. The other cars on the track were getting farther and farther ahead. Yet Bobby wanted a major repair job, a new engine installed. It would take most me-

Bobby Allison is in his "office" ready to "go to work."

chanics several hours to change an engine. The race was only going to last for another hour or so.

Still, racing mechanics are like racing drivers. They'll do almost anything to stay in a race. They don't quit. The mechanics started to make the engine change with Bobby Allison's help. Even Penske pitched in to help. In less than an hour the job was finished. Roaring and gunning the new engine, Bobby raced back onto the track.

He didn't win, but he didn't lose by much either. And he was still running hard at the end of the race, passing other cars.

Bobby Allison is a handsome driver. His black hair now has touches of gray, but he is still very good looking. In 1977 he was forty-one years old. He has four children, two boys and two girls. He never thinks about retiring from the fast sport he loves.

Bobby is often invited to race in the famous IROC (International Race of Champions) races. These are races between the top twelve drivers in the world. The drivers race in sports cars as equal as they can be. Another driver not in the races gets the cars ready. Nobody knows who will drive which car until just before the races start. Drivers win points in each race.

There are four of these races every year among the twelve drivers. Different tracks are used so that everything stays as equal as possible. The driver with the most points after the last race is the winner for that year. Bobby Allison has placed very high in the points in IROC races.

An Allison pit stop is a frantic affair. Gas is dumped in, tires changed, and even the windshield is cleaned.

But just to race in a race like that is an honor to most drivers, including Bobby. These are the best drivers from all types of racing and from around the world.

When he was seventeen years old, Bobby Allison almost died in a boating accident. He was testing a new outboard motor at a lake in Wisconsin. The boat turned over out in the middle of the lake.

That wasn't the worst of it. The temperature was only fifteen degrees above zero. The water was almost freezing. Allison was being dragged under by the weight of his soaked clothes.

Then ice began to form on his head and face. He was near death when he struggled up on shore. Luck was with him. The nearest house was owned by a doctor and a registered nurse. The nurse was at home. She knew just what to do and Allison's life was saved.

The racing career of Bobby Allison has not been all smooth. He started like most other young drivers. At first he didn't win, then he began to win a few races. That is how it almost always works.

But usually the driver then wins races regularly. Allison's career has been up and down. He wins for awhile, then he loses for awhile. It has not been easy.

In 1974 things were not going all that well, though Bobby was trying his best. Then at the end of the year he won the famous Los Angeles Times Grand Prix for stock cars. That started his winning streak. He won the next race (in 1975) at Riverside Raceway, then a 125-mile race at Daytona in Florida. Then he won the Rebel 500 race and the Southern 500 at Darlington, South Carolina. These are two of stock car racing's most important events.

That year of 1975, Bobby won a total of four races. He placed second three times, third once, and fourth and fifth twice. It was a fine, money-winning year.

But then in 1976, in thirty races, he never won a single one. Not that stock car drivers like Allison ever lose very badly. That year he placed in the top five 15 times and in the top ten 19 times during the thirty races. Even though he didn't win a race, he still made more than $190,000 in prize money. Losing like *that* isn't too bad.

Bobby Allison is one of the drivers who turned to driving his own cars rather than cars owned by somebody else. He built them in his garage in Hueytown, Alabama. Then he drove them on tracks all around the country. You have to pay all the expenses but you get to keep all the prize money instead of sharing it with an owner.

Stock cars aren't cheap, either. Usually if you

Two racing superstars, Bobby Allison (right) and two-time Indy winner, Johnny Rutherford.

are the owner you must put much of the winnings back into the car to keep it running well. Take stock car engines, for example. You need several of them for each car, and they cost more than $10,000 *each*.

"The modern 358 Grand National [stock car] engine is really a piece of equipment," says car owner Bobby Allison. "As much as a USAC Indy engine or a Formula One engine."

In 1978 Bobby finally won the stock car race that many fans think is the most important one of all, the Daytona 500.

Win or lose, Bobby is an all-time champion in stock car racing. If he is entered in his own car or in somebody else's car, he is favored to win. At Indy or in Sportsman or Grand National stock cars, he is hard to beat. He is truly one of auto racing's real superstars.

6
AL AND BOBBY UNSER

The 1974 California 500 at Ontario was a wild race. The lead changed twenty-one times as the racers battled for victory. But there was something special about the lead changes in this race for Indy-type championship cars.

Eight times the lead was held by one driver. Seven times it was held by another driver—all in the same race. Most special of all, these two drivers were brothers.

They were the Unser brothers, Bobby and Al. They were from a racing family. The Unsers are probably the most famous racing family of all. It is unusual when other brothers race against

Bobby (left) and Al Unser

each other. But the fans are used to seeing the Unsers together on a race track.

In that Cal 500 in 1974 the brothers were almost side by side near the end of the race. Coming out of the final turn, Bobby was leading Al by one car-length. After 500 speeding miles, they were nose to tail. Down the long straightaway they raced, engines roaring. When the checkered flag fell, Bobby was only *.58 second* ahead of his brother, Al.

The father of the boys was a racer and mechanic. Their uncles were racers. Their older brother, Jerry, was a racer until he was killed in a racing accident at Indy. Bobby and Al Unser grew up in racing. They never thought much about being in any other business. They just naturally turned to racing because their family had always been in the sport.

"I never thought about what else I might do in life," said Al. "I really don't know what else I could do. I grew up in racing. I do it well. I make good money at it."

Al Unser has become one of racing's millionaires. So has Bobby, who says, "You never know how long you'll live, so the thing is to make the most of it while you can."

Bobby Unser, in car No. 2 (seen on the left), is side by side with Mark Donohue, in car No. 66, at the start of the 1971 Indy 500. Directly behind Bobby in fourth place is Al Unser, who went on to win.

Good racing drivers are not afraid to race. They don't think about death. They feel that when they are going to die, they are going to die, no matter what they are doing. So they might as well enjoy racing.

Both Unser boys feel that way. They do not worry about high-speed driving on a race track. They do their best and enjoy it.

What happens when a driver is killed by racing? "His time was up," the other drivers say. They believe that the man would have died, no matter what he was doing. They think he just happened to be racing on that day.

The Unser boys are best known in Indy-type racing. They are champions in this dangerous class of racing. Bobby won the 1974 California 500 just ahead of Al. He also won the 1976 California 500. He won the Indy 500 two times, in 1968 and 1975. That's four wins in 500-mile races.

But from the results of 500-mile races, the brothers are almost equal in skill. For Al Unser is also a winner of several 500-mile races. These are the toughest races of all, according to many drivers. Al won the Indy 500 in 1970 and again in

1971. He won the Pocono 500 in 1976. He won the California 500 in 1977. Then he won the Indy 500—the big one at Indianapolis Speedway—for the third time in 1978.

Al and Bobby do not look like brothers. At least not until you get very close to them. Bobby is taller and thinner. He is the older brother. He was born in 1934. It was natural for him to start driving race cars at age fifteen. Most of his family was doing it.

By the time he was sixteen years old, Bobby had become the Modified Stock Car Champion in his home state of New Mexico. When he won the local championship again the next year, people knew he was going to be a famous driver someday.

Everybody in racing knows about Bobby and the Pike's Peak Hill Climb race. Drivers try to see who can get to the top of the mountain the quickest. Bobby won the race in 1956 when he was twenty-two years old. He kept right on winning the famous hill climb until 1964. That year another driver snapped his winning streak. The other driver was Bobby's younger brother, Al.

But by then Bobby was ready for Indianapolis.

It was not a happy year, though. Bobby was involved in the fiery crash that took the lives of Dave MacDonald and Eddie Sachs. Bobby's car was out of the race on the second lap.

Al Unser is the "baby" of the family. He was born in 1939. He is shorter than Bobby and has a handsome, innocent-looking appearance. His face is crinkled with lines of laughter. Al doesn't seem to take racing's dangers very seriously at all.

"If nothing happens [at a race] you go home when its over . . . and if it does, you don't," he says with a casual shrug.

Al also began racing in his home town in modified stock cars. Then while still in his teens he moved to Pike's Peak, known as "Unser's Hill" in Colorado. In his first race up the hill in 1960, Al finished in second place. The winner was his brother, Bobby.

Al missed a chance to be the first three-times-in-a-row winner at Indy when his racer failed only 14 laps from the end of the 1972 Indy race. He had won the race the two years before.

Bobby spoke of the success of the brothers with a writer. "You get to the point where you

Bobby Unser in one of the Indy-type cars he has driven so successfully.

enjoy success. Today, you can walk down a street in any town in America and ask the first five people you meet 'Have you ever heard of Bobby and Al Unser?'

"How many will answer yes? Two or three, probably. There aren't that many people or athletes living that are so well known. It's a great feeling and I'm glad I've earned such recognition. I love people, racing fans, and I love to talk about cars."

The brothers are in demand as racers. They are also in demand for other events. Both are excellent public speakers.

Bobby Unser followed in the footsteps of his father. His son is now doing the same. Bobby Unser, Jr., is now racing up Pike's Peak and in oval track races around the country. Does Bobby, the father, enjoy his own son's racing?

"I think it's like what my own dad went through, or like what my mother went through. Watching Bobby drive is the hard part for me."

Al's teen-aged son, Al Unser, Jr., is already a New Mexico state champion in go-kart racing. The Unsers have always been a racing family. They intend to keep on racing.

Everybody knew the Unser brothers' mother as "Mom" Unser. She was a wonderful lady who followed her sons' careers after their father died. She once said, "Racing is this family's life. We've had our tragedies, but what family hasn't? I don't blame racing, I love racing. I root for both of my boys and I root for all the boys." Mom Unser died in 1976, but before then she was well-known in big-time auto racing circles.

Bobby Unser's first victory at Indianapolis was

Al Unser in one of the Parnelli Jones Indy-type cars.

one that had the fans on their feet. He was running in second place behind Joe Leonard near the end of the race. Leonard was driving one of the turbine racers owned by Andy Granatelli.

Very near the end the turbine failed and pulled off the track. Bobby sped past.

"Let's go, Bobby," he said to himself. "Let's go while the sun is shining." And he did. He drove the final laps to his first great victory at the

Speedway. But he was forced to drive directly through the wreckage from his brother's crash during that same race.

Al was not hurt in that 1968 crash. By 1970 it was his turn at the Indy 500. It might have happened in 1969 but Al was hurt while riding a motorcycle and missed the big race. He didn't miss the 1970 race, though.

Al was assigned to drive Parnelli Jones' new Johnny Lightning Special. The car was very fast. Al drove it faster than anybody else during practice. He qualified faster and started the race from the pole position.

Then he drove faster than anybody else during the race, including his brother, Bobby. Al led the 200-lap race for 190 laps, including the final lap. He was more than 32 seconds ahead of second-place Mark Donohue at the finish.

The following year, 1971, he won again. He had become one of the very few two-times-in-a-row winners at the Speedway.

Meanwhile, Bobby's luck was fading. He had car problems in many races, and crashes in others. The brothers worry about each other when one or the other crashes. Otherwise they

Al Unser leads the field out of a crash at Riverside during an Indy-type race several years ago. Gordon Johncock is second. Spinning No. 25 is Lloyd Ruby.

race just as hard against each other as they do against the rest of the racers.

But if one crashes, the other watches until somebody gives him a signal that everything is OK. Once Bobby crashed and even though he had a bad headache and other pains, he limped out to the edge of the track as Al flashed past. He

107

waved to let his brother know he was OK.

"It was a comfort to me," Al recalls.

Then luck shifted again. Bobby began to win and Al began to lose. Still, by 1977, both brothers had become superstars in auto racing. No matter what they are driving, stock cars or Indy cars, they are favored to win. Both brothers think the Indy race is the most important of all. There are other 500-mile races, but Indy is *the* 500-mile race. It is the race that drives every racer on, always hoping and praying to win.

Jimmy Bryan was a racing champion years ago. He won the Indy 500 in 1958 after many years of trying. Jimmy was a tough-looking, cigar-smoking man with huge arms and a square jaw. Before he died in a racing crash, he said what most drivers believe.

"If you never win another dollar in racing the rest of your life, you will still be someone. When you're old and tired and scared and ready to die, you will still be someone who once won the 500."

That is what the Unsers believe. It is what they have both done. It is what they both hope to do again.

Bobby Unser won the rain-shortened Indy race in 1975. Al Unser placed third in the very fast race of 1977, the race won by A.J. Foyt to give him his fourth Indy 500. Bobby won the 1976 Cal 500 and Al went on to win the 1977 Cal 500 and the 1978 Indy 500. Bobby placed sixth in that race. Neither brother is yet "old and tired and scared and ready to die." Neither speaks of retirement.

The racing Unser brothers get better and better. By now they are both rich men. They mix with royalty, with big businessmen, with other millionaires. They are far from where they started, farm boys who didn't have much money at all.

Yet, deep down, they are still hard-working racing drivers. Al spoke for both brothers when he said, "We're still what we always were. We belong in the grease, getting sweaty, using our muscles."

INDEX

"All America" team, 84
Allison, Bobby, 9, 10, 15, 81-95
Allison, Donnie, 85, 88
American Auto Racing Writers and Broadcasters Association, 84
Andretti, Aldo, 18-21
Andretti, Mario, 8, 12, 14, 18-33, 36-37, 50, 61, 75, 80

Baker, Buddy, 85
Brabham, 12
Brands Hatch Circuit, 42
Branson, Don, 28
Brawner-Hawk Special, 22-23
British Grand Prix, 47-48
Bryan, Jimmy, 108

California 500, 32, 96-98, 100, 109
CAM 2 Matador, 88
Canadian Grand Prix, 50
CanAm, 10
Chevrolet, 10
Clark, Jim, 61

Coca-Cola Mercury, 81
Copersucar, 12
Coyote, 12, 62-63

Darlington, South Carolina, 86, 93
Daytona Speedway, 15, 56, 95
Depailler, Patrick, 44
DePaolo, Peter, 57
Dijon, France, 31
Dodge, 10
Donohue, Mark, 84, 98, 106
"Driver of the Year," 84
Dutch Grand Prix, 48

Eagle, 12
Ertl, Harold, 70

Federation Internationale de L'Automobile (FIA), 15
Ferrari, 13, 26, 29, 36, 70-73, 76, 79-80
Ferrari, Commendatore Enzo, 77
FIA, 15, 29, 44

Fittipaldi, Emerson, 45
Follmer, George, 84
Ford, 10, 21
Formula A, 26
Formula Ford, 40
Formula One, 9-15, 17, 25-34, 41, 49, 51, 73, 77
Formula Three, 10
Formula Two, 10, 41
Formula Vee, 10
Four-wheel drive, 22
Foyt, A. J., 11-12, 14, 23, 53-67, 84, 109
Foyt, A. J. (Tony), Sr., 66
French Grand Prix, 47

German Grand Prix, 47
Gilmore Special, 11
"Golden Eagles" prize, 84
Granatelli, Andy, 23-24, 105
Grand National division, 87, 94-95
Grand Prix, 27-28, 34, 46
Gurney, Dan, 12, 25
Guthrie, Janet, 65

Hesketh, Lord Alexander, 41-42, 45
Hesketh Racing Team, 42
Hill, Phil, 32
Hueytown, Alabama, 93
Hulman, Tony, 67
Hunt, James, 12, 35-52, 72, 75

Indianapolis Speedway, 9-12, 21-23, 53-67, 104-106
Indy 500, 9-15, 17, 21-22, 24-25, 32, 98-99, 100-102
International Race of Champions (IROC), 90
IROC, 90

Isaac, Bobby, 85
Italian Grand Prix, 32

Japan Grand Prix, 28-29, 36, 50, 75, 80
John Player Lotus, 27
Johncock, Gordon, 65, 107
Johnny Lightning Special, 106
Jones, Alan, 51
Jones, Parnelli, 12, 29, 62, 105, 106

Lauda, Niki, 12-13, 29, 36-37, 46-52, 68-80
Leonard, Joe, 84, 105
London, England, 76
Long Beach Grand Prix, 8, 29, 30, 44, 52
Los Angeles Times Grand Prix, 92
Lotus, 12, 22, 29
Lunger, Brett, 70-72

MacDonald, Dave, 60, 102
Madrid, Spain, 29
Mayer, Teddy, 45
McLaren, 12, 37-38, 45-49
Merzario, Art, 71-72
Meyer, Lou, 64
Michigan International Speedway, 81-85
Midget racing cars, 10, 25
Monte Carlo, Monaco, 12
Monza, Italy, 12
Mount Fuji (Japan), 34-37, 50

NASCAR, 16, 17, 81, 87
National Association for Stock Car Auto Racing (NASCAR), 16
National Driving Champion, 56

111

Nazareth, Pennsylvania, 21, 25
Nürburgring, Germany, 68, 70-73

O'Connor, Pat, 56
Offenhauser, 9, 10
"On the pole," 45
Ontario Motor Speedway, 12, 96-98
Oval track, 14, 20

Parnelli racing car, 12
Pearson, David, 85
Penske, Roger, 88-89
Petty, Richard, 16, 81-84
Pike's Peak Hill Climb, 101, 102
Pocono Speedway, 12, 101
Points system, 16

Questor Grand Prix, 26

"Race of Champions," 42
Rain tires, 14
Rebel 500, 93
Regazzoni, Clay, 51
Rindt, Jochen, 17
Riverside International Raceway, 15, 60-61, 85-86, 93, 106
Road course, 11
Rose, Mauri, 64
Ruby, Lloyd, 107
Rutherford, Johnny, 94

Sachs, "Fast Eddie," 58-60, 102
Scheckter, Jody, 29, 80
Shaw, Wilbur, 64
Silverstone Race Track, 39

South African Grand Prix, 26, 46
Southern 500, 93
Sports cars, 10
Sportsman division, 87, 95
Sprint cars, 10, 25
Stock cars, 10, 14, 17, 20-21, 61-62, 82, 84-86, 93-94

Talladega Speedway, 15
Trenton, New Jersey, 85
Turbine, 62, 105
Turbocharger, 9, 10, 12

United States Auto Club (USAC), 15-16
United States Grand Prix, 50
Unser, Al, 10, 15, 32, 65, 96-109
Unser, Al, Jr., 104
Unser, Bobby, 9-10, 15, 84, 96-109
Unser, Bobby, Jr., 104
Unser, Jerry, 98
Unser, "Mom," 104
USAC, 15-17, 24, 56, 94

Victoria Sporting Club, 76
Victory Lane (Indianapolis Speedway), 23
Victory Lane (Nazareth, Pennsylvania), 21

Watkins Glen, New York, 12, 50
Watson, John, 31
World Driving Championship, 25, 29, 33, 37, 45, 51, 68, 75, 80

Yankee 400, 81